Copyright © 2016 by Rebecca Counts Kahila
All Rights Reserved
ISBN:9781533359681

Farmer Joe had a farm. On that farm, he had a PROBLEM.

He had complained about the noise his animals made, but now all of the animals had stopped talking.

The ducks would not quack!

The chickens would not cluck!

The cows would not moo!

Even the rooster would not crow!

He had quacked.

He had mooed.

So, he went to the kitchen and asked his wife, "Honey, What do you do when your ducks won't quack and you quack and you quack but they won't quack back?"

And she said, "Here's what you do when your ducks won't quack, you love them anyway. They'll quack another day."

"Pshaw!" he thought, "That's silly. I think I'll ask my Brother Billy." So, he walked on down the road to his Brother Billy's farm.

"Hey, Brother Billy," he called as he reached the front porch of his brother's house. "I got a problem! What do you do when the chickens won't cluck? I cluck and I cluck. I even called them ducks, but they just won't cluck!"

Brother Billy laughed and said, "You don't call a chicken a duck. Then it really won't cluck! Here's what I do when the chickens won't cluck, I love them anyway. They'll cluck another day."

"Pshaw!" Farmer Joe shook his head. "I just don't see how that could help. I am going to ask our sister. She's a teacher, and she's got some sense.

He headed up the hill to Mary's school just as the children left for the day. "Hey, Miss Mary! I hope you're not feeling contrary because I got a problem." Joe called to his sister.

"You have a problem," she corrected. "I am good at problems, just as you suspected."

"Well, little sister," he asked politely, "What do I do when the rooster won't crow? I've shouted cock-a-doodle. I even called him a poodle! He just won't crow."

Miss Mary laughed and said, "You silly goose. Is your brain loose? Roosters have feelings too. Calling him a poodle just won't do. When that old rooster won't crow, just love him anyway. He'll crow another day!"

"That's what I have heard all day, every way I have turned," Farmer Joe complained.

As he trudged back down the road toward home, he decided, "I'll ask my neighbor, Farmer Jack. Jack's been farming since farming began. He'll know what to do to set things right again."

"Howdy, Jack," Joe said when he found his neighbor in the field. "I have a problem. What do you do when a cow won't moo, and you moo and you moo, but it just looks at you?"

Farmer Jack scratched his head and said, "Well, here's what I do when the cow won't moo, I feed her extra hay and I love her anyway. She'll moo another day."

"For goodness sakes!" Farmer Joe exclaimed. "I've heard the same thing all day. Love them anyway? Can that really make things OK? I guess I'll just have to see if it really is that easy."

When he reached the field in front of his house, he saw old Bess—his oldest, best, sweetest cow. Farmer Joe tucked his hat under his sleeve.

He strolled up to Bess, handed her some hay, and said, "I love you anyway."

Old Bess looked at him with her brown, watery eyes and mooed the biggest MOOO a cow ever mooed. Every animal on the farm heard Bess's call. The chickens ruffled their feathers and began clucking.

The ducks quacked so loudly that the pigs squealed. And the rooster, why the rooster crowed so much that Honey came running from the house to see what was the matter.

She gazed down the road to see her husband running to the house shouting, "I love them anyway!" Now every day, Farmer Joe works his farm smiling.

He listens to the ducks quacking, the chickens clucking, the cows mooing, and the rooster crowing. They make a lot of noise, but he loves them anyway. (And he never forgets to give old Bess a little extra hay.)

Made in the USA
Columbia, SC
01 April 2021